Le Femme Tácita

Poetry 1995 - 2019

2nd edition with changes published January 2020

FEEL MORE

To Judy, finally.

To young me, thank you.

To future me, here I come.

Outline

Before..9

The Beginning..........................11

THE POSITIONS

on Man...15
on Man and Society.....................17
on Man and the Universe.............19
on Society....................................21
on the Universe...........................23
on God...25
on Woman....................................27
on Woman and Children..............29
on Woman and Man.....................31
on Woman and Society.................33
on Woman and The Universe........35

THE REFLECTIONS

Nature..39
Sex..41
Beauty..43
Chemistry.....................................45
Experience....................................47
Memory...49
Knowledge....................................51

Intuition.............................53
Art....................................55
Music................................57
Wisdom.............................59

THE PLAN

Freedom.............................63
Understanding.....................65
Forgiveness........................67
Compassion........................69
Education............................71
Civilization..........................73
Architecture........................75
Cultivation..........................77
Exploration.........................79
Deviation............................81
Evolution............................83

The End.............................85

The Silent Woman

Before

       Thank you to Judy Moss, my first God, my motherland and heart. Thank you to Isis for her strength and Nola for her wisdom and Eko for his joy. Thank you to the countless writers and musicians whom I love and hold so close to my heart, who have gifted me all the swagger and the rhythms and the sounds – my Gods, thank you for the pictures you make so real with sounds and patterns and talent and heart and soul. Thank you for being here - may we walk together in grace.

-   Dunmore, Erie, Mount Oliver,
and Pittsburgh, Pennsylvania
1995 to 2019

Isis

Isis has blue eyes.
They are deep and knowing,
and although they haven't seen a full year yet
they are here and ready to do business.

She comes clean.
She can stare at you for hours
and not expect a damn thing.
Our relationship is completely appreciative.
I love her honesty and what she loves
she keeps as her secret,
but lately she says 'mum'
and I know what she means.

She makes this world
and the men in charge look small,
a baby girl towering over billions of dollars
and billions of war-hardy men
and sweeping it all away.

She will outlive me AND them,
and her world is and will be free.

The Beginning

Daylife

For winds to breathe a weary sound
    and leaves to rustle as Earth turns round
    and night to come like a woman's whisper
    and life to leave in unison.

For black to fall in velvet shade
    and moon to contrive with star-strewn wave
    and silent control like a sealed-up letter
    and peace to reign completely.

For trees to sing in nestling calls
    and shadows to lift from dew-drop dolls
    and orb to rise like love's crescendos
    and day to greet in harmony.

For solace comes when least rehearsed
    and creations do tinker at our source
    as a life completes its circle leaving
    the mind to dine with sanity.

Vision 1

Dreamy when I was young
almost real dreams
I floated down many steps
felt feet fumbling
but I did not tumble,
just floated down with fumbling feet.
Did I try to pull it off in real life, too?
If so I never faltered

Must have turned dream into reality
with little girl thoughts.

The Positions

I. A Position on Man

Eternal Ambition

At first devoid of form
then unleashed into this world
to grow comfortable temporarily.

A motherless child are ye,
my son,
for it is not our earth that lies within you
but the heavens and those stars flickering beyond reach.

A constant struggle lies straight out before you
to encompass and penetrate
all that is around you;
to become outside of yourself,
to conquer and battle and evolve.
And your sun belies great depth
about you.

Heed the old advice of sages:
Remember your mothers and fathers,
sisters and brothers,
and keep close to your heart
the love you know to be true.

Before your first step is laid down on the path,
the work has already begun
and finished.

Fill your whole intention
with light and love,
without judgement or justification.

And truly understand that the next moment
is a phantom of your optimistic expectations,
not guaranteed to fulfil its open invitation.

II. A Position on Man and Society

America 2004

Look around you.

The people in the street are still starving,
for real.
No oxygen or knowledge,
no clean water or fresh meals.
No leaders for the people
only for the richest few.
And the American Dream died 20 years ago,
I know you saw it, too.

If you're not addicted to the street
you have a steady prescription.
Something to go to sleep, to digest,
one that handles all afflictions.
A woman or a man who suffers
right there next to you,
long ago convinced themselves
that they were just like you.

There is some hatred in your heart
you must accept and let move through you
if you want to rid yourself
of your self-inflicted voodoo.
It's not tricky or expensive
and it'll make you feel real good.
Not just the first time,
son,
don't fool yourself.
There is no price for truth.

III. A Position on Man
and the Universe

The Worked

The lie is a pain in the neck.

The desire to lie is the bent neck,
wilted to the weight
and complete darkness of the world.

Why would you hide from such shining beauty?

Light thrown in reaching waves
and all around, insatiable sound
stretches to no end
to permeate all points
with honesty too magnificent to deny.

■■■

There is a voice within who speaks to you of freedom.
The masses develop only to reject.
For them there is no cause, mere justification.
They think there is no choice but theirs,
denying even that they are denying.

IV.   A Position on Society

Pittsburgh, August 3rd, 2001

an Ozone Action Day
          was called
                two days ago
                          the sky was thick,
                    took a trip outside
to see
          the new smog
            hovering contentedly
                                about third-story
level
                    closing in
              on all its
                          earthly fellows.

so we ran into the conditioned office air
                    into Chinese restaurants and churches
                          and skyscrapers with spinning
restaurants
                          poised on their
                                    haughty
heights.

Money Problems

Can't say that it looks cool.
Only know one or two
new-money non-fools.
Figure those cats know the rules.
Like it's sad we gotta call class
a classic throwback forgotten hit.
Wish they all knew who's still,
will be and been running it.
Quiet thunder brings the reign –
superior quality A+ King shit.

V. A Position on the Universe

Blink

Forever in cool shadows
have I remained entranced
with the idea of a memory
in creation born again.
(Quietly within myself sparks fly into form.)

I whisper slowly quietly
a song that has no tune
and gather the emotions
that continue enclosed to burn.
(And quietly within myself a being slowly turns.)

I grasp the future tightly
but must look back once more
to fathom the eternal winding path
that is unknown.
(And quietly within myself the magic one is born.)

The High Priestess

Twelve years of sabotage
and I was supposed to fold.
I was supposed to be bound
with knots I tied myself
to hold me
to days and nights so scary
that telling someone in words
doesn't work,
doesn't fit those nights right.

But I knew he never had the right.
So I did the other thing.
I sat still and covered myself with light,
and covered my children,
and we hid there in plain sight.

Then I found my voice
and called the wolves on him
and now we watch them feast.
I'm telling you nothing even looks the same
from within this kind of peace.

VI. A Position on God

Children

Children are not afraid
but not because
they do not know fear.

A young heart sees fear
and sees beyond it,
does not drown in its
routines or sorrows,
but beats its fresh blood
without limit.

Prayer

Small steps, Lord.
Avoid all sharp stones.
Gaze deeply at smooth pebbles.
Blow away wind-fallen debris
and revel in harmless puddles
dotting your path.
Small steps, Lord,
and we will make it just fine.

Thank you God
for showing me
everything that I need to see
in order to know
everything that I need to know.

Thank you God
for blessing us & protecting us,
and for keeping us always
happy, healthy, safe and strong.

VII. A Position on Woman

Light

A match never lit can never compare
        to a match snuffed out, which, in turn
        cannot compare to a match that lights a candle
        and dissolves itself in that flame,
        giving up and going on,
        putting to rest sudden inspiration
        in return for a substantial end.

Dream and waking life hang suspended
        in weighted globes,
        moving through complete
        peaceful darkness,
        a traveling infant's sleep.

Constantly spinning orb flashes sorrow, confusion
        shows no escape to the sad soul
        still stubbornly clinging,
        the nightmare to end only in a new dream
        from where the dreamer shall never wake,
        to show him what he has made.

Serenity now comes not with the knowledge
        that all is aright
        but with discovery of self's
        own timeless illusion,
        finally a true equanimity
        between memory and life's confusion,
        as now one can see everything has not
        ever existed
        nothing is always one's only companion.

VIII.   A Position on Woman and Children

Cool Sleep, August 1988

I sat on the green shag rug
wanting to tear the loops
apart
with my little girl hands.
The TV was too close
to my eyes, but I wanted
to see everything.
I watched Nickelodeon,
losing myself to Family
Double Dare
and the Brady Bunch.
My dog slept heavy,
his head on my lap,
nostrils streaming
warm breath onto my bare
thighs.
It was summer: I was
sweating.

My mother was upstairs,
needing to be alone,
coping with the migraine
she had since the night
before.
She came home late,
a little before my father
who stumbled inside while
she tucked me in,
telling me to pretend I'd been
asleep for hours.
She tucked up the too-warm
blanket
and tried to kiss me, but
her breath smelled like my
dog's

and I was afraid of her face
with her makeup smeared all
over.
She got in the shower,
and I tried to close my eyes
but the noise was so loud,
the noise of water and crying.
My father, downstairs,
taking water from the sink to
make tea,
battled my mother for the
same supply.
I fell asleep with Teddy in my
arms
and I was a good mother.

I remember I slept badly that
night,
and the next day I was
hungry,
and maybe even the day after
that.
My father went golfing
every day that summer,
my mother didn't talk much,
and I started sleeping out in
the yard.
It was cooler there.

IX. A Position on Woman and Man

7324 Days

Alarm at 5:30 interrupted some kind of good dream
that had kept me interested
even up until almost-waking.
After long sleepy shower fell back
into cool room and toasty sheets,
still warm and damp with damp chilly hair.
Sleep came too easy again,
and the warmth of one sheet, a comforter
and a man's sleeping thigh drove the sail
deeply into dream again.
Sluggish waking, clock displays 6:30,
small sleepy conversation and long clean fingernails
to run over his back.
Two children exposed to all time.

Shots

We can talk about
the collective unconscious
about dollar sign belt buckles
and big flashy watches,
about how the game
thrusts its way in
just to bust us down,
leaves a trust so thin
that half the time
your love shots
don't even hit my rim.

X. A Position on Woman and Society

Woman's Work

I know what it is to carry a tray
piled high with glasses and reminders
that I am your servant,
sometimes less than that.
You are always right.

I know what it is to drop things,
to go home with swollen feet,
to know hot water with salts
and forget about dinner.

I know what it is to stand all day
in factory-bred heat, pull sheets of metal
from unforgiving conveyor belts,
and taste the copper in my throat
long into my sleep.

I know what it is to be told to lie down,
to pretend to be your mother,
your daughter, the girl you knew in high school
who you could never touch,
or just another whore willing to please,
to pretend that I like it,
to remember innocence
hazy and years behind,
and how the value of money
splits between my thighs.

I know what it is to care for men,
women, children, fish,
dry-clean-only suits in the sink,
to watch you sleep,
and to serve you breakfast in my bed
if only to keep you there a little while longer.

I know what it is to give.

XI. A Position on Woman and the Universe

Solar System Mistress

Graceful, tender and wise
soft skin, silken hair, open eyes.
Woman models mother nature
in all of her ways,
nurtures life through this death
and still always remains
with a peaceful placid face
of understanding and compassion.
But inside our hearts fire burns,
sweet attraction.

■■

My heart's true darkness
in contrast to your light
withholds nothing,
expands in passion.
Planets and moons for my wristbands
and earth and heaven for yours.

A solar system mistress
for your infinite desire.
A partner in completion,
our souls consuming fire.
Together our circle forms
          a union
as old as our histories tell.

Two into nothing,
my truth and yours
to dispel any hate.

The Reflections

I. Nature

The Purpose

You will be turned on.
You will be delighted.
You will follow that good feeling
more and more every day...

And you will see more and more
of what brings you that feeling...
And you will turn others on
just because you become that light.

And the world becomes that light.

Cartographer

Songs like treasure maps
Fell hard to follow your tracks
So now I'm attached

II.Sex

Selfie

They don't understand
why I waste my time
a settled-down woman shouldn't bother
They find
me strange I know
but you know 'bout my why
I do all this work
'cause I'm trying to climb
And if all that I face
at the end of the line
is a worst-case scenario
of dying while fine
Well then vain though it be
if I take it it's mine

And until then I sweat
for the way that my waist
and my thighs cut the eyes
and your mind blurs the stakes
I can swing out some hips
that will fill up the space
above your lap and you'd clap
or even cover your face
But you can't do that, can you
with both hands slamming the pace.
Mmmm!!!
And when you awake
from that hero lover's rest
you'll have a full perfect plate
of what you say you want
next.

III. Beauty

Short Poems

Hanging up her raincoat
leaking nighttime's raindrops
flooding day's desires.

Sunlight glistens
on golden strands
fair skin
dimpled flesh
uncovered and vulnerable
in the reflection of the bearer.

Glimmering stars see
your hand upon my blouse
emitting silky love.

Heels

3" and up
and people will stop
and ask me
if I am a model.
I like that a lot
'cause I know that
I'm not
but I feel like I can
if I want to.

IV. Chemistry

Hands

To shake away your starry eyes
that night we stood
together in a field
of clover.

To escape your taste,
tangerine, abrupt,
lingering in my mouth
long after my hands
closed my door on you.

To explain your warm hands
on my blouse, fallen open,
your urgent touch
making me doubt
love's approaching free-fall.

That is why I write.

Like Kerouac

I love a good conversation
vibing, relating.
I get it with strangers
in real life in the daytime,
small packages of the sublime.
Most days I guess that only I
can feel it.
These moments end pleasantly --
twice I've kindly denied
a proposal to wed.
Hah! True but useless.
Still my time is well-fed.

V. Experience

Insipid

A quick tour of this dream reveals little.
Still so many of us choose to
illude-undate our days
with the happenings and dramatics
we assume must be part
of the people package.
Why can't we ever convince ourselves
that no one out here is experiencing this conversation,
this slanty-eyed bus stare,
or this ride to work in the morning the same way?
It is only the sum of all our perceptions
that proposes any reality,
so powerful that no one has to agree with it.
So where exactly
are all the multitudes
you'll compose about yourself
when brought to stand and face
the depths of your true fantasy?

Larry with the Picked Out Fro

You knew you were my first man
I knew you were sweet on me
I really, really liked holding your hand
I liked the way you smiled at me
and how when I was scared
you cared for me
At eight years old though,
I didn't know how long
our friendship would carry me.
And I can't remember your last name,
and I don't know where you went,
and I hope you stayed alive and free
and I hope you kept your smile
and maybe you've had a girl,
and maybe you've thought of me.
I'll always love us Larry,
as silly as that may seem.

VI. Memory

Shiver

A February morning
alone in the house,
chilled-bone trembling
with the pre-dawn rhythm
of my solo breathing.
Worn floorboards,
Forever locked hinges.
The house settles
into the earth,
I into a chair.

I pull up the blankets
stare out the window.
A world still quiet
rolling forward.

Remembering this full house,
the empty giggles of
my parents' friends
who boozed and danced while we
watched behind banisters,
wearing only our footsie pajamas.
The long Thanksgiving dinners when
we sat, bibbed and alone in the
kitchen, catching
glimpses of cranberries
glistening on the dining room table.
The picture of my mother rocking in
the chair that we gave her, alone with
her grief for this forgotten house,
wondering if she's missed
as much as she misses.

White knuckled
I grip the blanket
and shiver.

The snow rolls on forever.
There wasn't enough time
for snow angels or forts,
for bedtime stories, for hugs
and kisses goodnight.
We could never compete with the
raised newspaper, or the lipstick
stained mug, or his
starched white collar's
still intimidation.

Dad would say, "My children will
grow to be of strong character,"
but he never taught us
how to be strong.
We taught ourselves as we crept
through the woods after curfew,
stumbled drunkenly through
briars and brambles, guided by
moonlight to our house on the hill,
developed a plan, sobered up
in case of confrontation, nervous
as hell and loving every minute.

The sun rises
and I crawl back to bed.
The furnace wakes up
floors below,
stirring chilled memories
that never seem to sleep.

VII. Knowledge

Walking Out of Time
(on the visit of the Drepung-Loseling monks)

Bewildered eyes peer into me,
searching for an answer I cannot share.
They are brown, clear and
almond shaped,
holding knowledge and frustration
captive behind glass,
trying to stretch inside to my soul.

His furrowed brow wants
me to understand
that he cannot stay until next year
or September, or tomorrow,
that he cannot write to tell me
he is okay, ever,
that he is leaving for his peaceful home
and that I cannot come.

His lips, innocent of mine,
of everyone's,
part and whisper comforting syllables
of trust, responsibility, devotion
in his native way,
mixing my language and his
rendered unintelligible
by religion and desire.

Still my fingers cradle his neck,
wander over his shaved skull
while he tells me why this is wrong,
why he can't and I shouldn't.

His robe clings to my dress,
stately red against flowered print,
friction making static stars

flash like lightning.
His hands caress my shoulder blades
while I plead, selfishly
needing to know that he loves me
and would be with me if he could be.

His lips are stopped by my finger,
slightly pressing as my heart slows.
His untouchable face leans over me
as he kisses my temples
softly, like dew caressing the grass
beneath us.
These are your most sacred spots,
he says,
It is here you will remember me.

His hands withdraw silently,
folding themselves into a steeple
before him,
into a gesture of distance.
He turns, walking in worn sandals
to a future without me,
walking in worn sandals
away from our history.

VIII. Intuition

Magic

My guess is the magic's
as real as the news
that we are allowed
to make up the rules
Lines in the sand
and what sand does is shift
perceptions of order
and what's allowed in.

The Portalist

I gotta keep the vision
Me and you in a kitchen
Uniform for cooking
something delicious
panties and a tank top
got your eyes lit &
you steady sipping
over at the table sittin while
I'm plating up the mission
wetting your lips twice
bare naked ambition.

IX. Art

In Flight

No tall ivory tower
with a dragon on guard,
no.
They tried to get me up there once
and this is how that goes:

On the first night the dragon lay
sleeping at my toes,
and the second day, as soon as we ate
I climbed on his back and he flew
me away.

There's no structure that can keep me,
no.
I have to try, I have to go.
The queens that came before me know
our power is greater,
we show off our souls.
Resting here only to live in the dream,
returning with all that we learn
while we're there
drop it off in the daylight
then what's real is clear.

Horses run faster with me on their back.
I see the whole picture:
liquor gets stronger,
men suddenly richer.
Focus perfect like twilight,
shadows relieved in the mixture.

Like that.

X.Music

More Groove

All I wanna do is
zooma zoom zoom zoom.
Bra comin off
when there's bars in the room.
Say there she blows
and I see your harpoon
raisin up mighty stiff
like it's claimin high noon
then boom!
& everybody freeze
for a minute or two.
Body beggin for a few more
measures of the groove.
Another inch, swear there's room.
Lay it down and pretty soon
I'll be swearing that it's you.
Sir, I gotta have that food.
Nobody do it like you do.
Nobody do it like you do.

XI. Wisdom

Learning to Love

Dim sunlight streams through the
antique lace curtains
which are billowing now,
entertaining a sudden breeze.
The light
cast in fanciful patterns on the wall
now moves,
changing form
changing reality.
I wonder if he noticed things
like that,
like how his watch-glass curves
and casts brilliant streams of
orange
purple
hazy green
when turned at the right angle,
at my angle
as it is now.
Now in this deathwatch
this thick shroud of sleep
that I hope will take him
mercifully
without pain
I do not know
if he would notice the perfect symmetry
of my tears
or the sudden spots of red
high on my face.
But if I pointed them out
if I showed him exactly how the blood vessels
cast their raw color,
or how unseeable prisms
appearing from nowhere
show us how limited our sight really is,

or how lace
may be taken for granted
and placed under an urn
or a vase or a candy dish
where it can't breathe,
flow
live...
I'm sure he would understand
this complexity
like he understood why I needed to be saved
from the monsters and the demons
and the men and the world,
like he understands that I will be alone...
Even now his frail body
shuddering with each breath
gives new life
and old knowledge to me
I wish I could tell him once more that
I love him
tell him I'll be all right...
I'm watching my father die
and I am not sure
that anyone ever taught me to love
more than this.

The Plan

I. Freedom

Affair

Still I close my eyes and free my mind
Your fingers grazing up my thigh
while somewhere my head
is still down up topside
your touch is a secret
You're drawing our line
For the eyes I laugh
slap the table sometimes
keeps it seeming sly
Like none of this is biding time
Your fingers in my mind
I'd come to a hundred lines
All inside one night
if one night's all the time
that you and I could oblige

Cheers

Here's to who you are
who you started out as
how you never changed.
Here's to who you are
without saying you are someone's
wife or husband
girlfriend or boyfriend
mother or father
partner or boss.
Here's to you
and to the song you hear
inside your head when you wake
and here's to how you let that song
guide your whole entire day.

II.Understanding

Slither

From two years old I could see the air
Blue and green and pink bubbles
swirling like liquid all around me
I could see it whenever I got tired
and so then I learned to play with it
Turn it off and on during the day

Most of the air is good but some
of it moves like a slither
and wants to harm us – I can tell
All the other air moves away from it
Like that piece is a shark and
Those slithery pieces made me
afraid to see

Two months ago I was finally brave enough
to apply this vision to a dark person
and I saw nothing there – cooled lava
with some read sparks sliding along
A slither in human form

4 A World Removed

Back to reality, then.

What is reality?

Reality is what we make it.

III. Forgiveness

On the Block

We got some cool people
down on my block
Across the street we got Mike
He's like everyone's pops
Lots of dudes climb his porch
to sit and gather his thoughts
I tend to find his wife Char
when I'm at a loss
and I now need to know
how to make it still go
So over the years she's let me know
to make it to 20, 25, 30 or more
to keep a tight, strong, loving
functioning real family home
Exactly means always letting it go
either fast or slow depends on you,
you know,
but girl, you just have to let that shit go
Forgiveness ain't shit if it's easy, you know
While we pass a joint between us
and her wine supply gets leaner
and my vision, well, of course,
just gets sharper and meaner
As she indicates the other side
of forgiving him is freedom
And I like the sound of
not being bound by just
sitting home and grieving.

IV. Compassion

Beheld

Puzzle pieces gently falling
from a box hence tipped,
hand-painted with delicate precision
formulated to command a life lived.
Scattered over a field of dreams,
gently swaying to the songs of the earth,
quick! Find the corner pieces and set them out
far away from the civilized world.

■■■

The day has come now
when we must start to build,
throw out the manual
and on our own live.

With straight sides and tangled edges,
we will fight until the end.

When the day is completed
and the grasses are still,
the children will return to the earth,
and under a billion stars' lights
we will finish what was begun
in a land far away
and a time left unknown.

V. Education

May I Speak to You?

At this point in the game
even children understand
that liars can't lead
and deaf ears won't ever hear you,
screaming or no screaming.
Educate yourself and you'll only have yourself
to blame,
or thank,
for your current situation.
True power, true freedom, too.
One encompassing simple solution.

EMPOWERED PEOPLE ARE NOT CONFUSED.

Dedicated to Shel Silverstein

Life :

You always know the answer
in the beginning and the end,
so while you're in the middle,
you should be your own best friend.

VI. Civilization

The King and I

Only trying to add, sir,
never depreciate.
It's what you've been doing for me
and I'm about that fair,
righteous exchange.
Still
I can get real and shyly admit
that though I try to match,
your gifts to me have had
no noticeable limit.
So
competitive to the bones
I open some more
and more words flow through
as they've tended to do.
But new
for this grown woman I've become
is the extra-sweaty workouts,
poses, it's fun
to jam along and in the middle
of your song
I get flashes of my back
against a brick wall
and you're asking if we can
do it together.

That shit is so right on.

VII. Architecture

Doctrine

The space between
someone's expectation of you
and what is real
is a window of opportunity
for you.

Make the most out of
the moment
when the person holds
both images of you
and capitalize on this
distortion:

As soon as you see
the hole in the moment,
drive yourself through.

Battlefield

Angels are God's warriors.
Most people think we live in heaven.
But there are no battles in heaven.
The only battles are right here...
...inside your mind.
That is why we fight for you here.
Be forever aware of our love.

VIII.   Cultivation

The Gardner

My lifetime is writing
so when I hear Dear Whoever
sometimes I start crying.
Letter for an old friend who didn't die
but when they grew
they changed inside
& a lot of good got left behind.

And how many notebooks did I stop
filling up halfway through?
All of em,
even stopped writing once, too.
But I knew already then
whose voice was coming through.

And if I want to breathe now
then I had better make a way,
find a lonely narrow lane
& give myself space,
and write a new day for me
each and every day.

So thanks always for receiving
all the things I write to you.
Possibly anything you do,
when it lands in my pond
makes a deep splash,
leaves a ripple or two.

IX. Exploration

Above Around Below Beneath

What if I told you
I've slipped just beneath here
and battled what lives there

how that thing was here and not here
the whole time

how it wasn't the only one

how I saw them when I leaned into my faith,

how the application of faith changed my vision.

Sex Magic

I hope sometimes when we talk
and you see my pictures
that your mouth drops open,
definitely you lean in, you zoom in.
Maybe sometimes your face looks pained
'cause it makes you want to touch
and every now and again
I hope you lean back in your chair,
clasp your hands together and raise them to the sky,
throw your head back and say thank you
to whatever you thank up there.
'Cause I'm so thankful for you,
for what you do, for how you do it,
how consistently high-quality you are.
Thank you, King.

X. Deviation

Fight Seen

Only notice the darkness
to note it's receding
Don't give any monsters
an edge by believing
Call it victory
when you leave them bleeding
shadow blood everywhere
evaporates to the ceiling
A crumpled figure left
alone, unsure
and barely breathing
Without your heart in their hands
there is no heart in their pleadings
And now you know the seat and power
of your believing

Queen of Swords

Somebody begging for a showdown?
Well, I pray you brought some bricks
'cause that funny footed feeling
got your split tongue playing tricks
on the room's only pair of ears
who still can listen to your shit.
Both are yours, blessed be,
it's not too late to make a switch
seeing how under-armed you came tonight
to step to this boss bitch.

XI. Evolution

Hardcover

I was finding my way when you found me
You needed me to be strong
The kids needed us to be strong
So I was strong for you
And we were strong for them
But I fucked up and got scared
And tried to have you all to myself
Forgot that you were alone before we
Didn't want to think you'd ever
be alone without me
I was scared of everyone who you loved
who wasn't me.
And I don't blame you for finding happiness
with others
You have a gift to share and you should
I have been angry at myself
for compromising what I want
in order to keep you
And I have been angry at you
for knowing that I would
But no more
Please be happy wherever with whomever
doing whatever you choose
And one day maybe
we can reconnect
and share stories of all the things
we've done and seen and been since then
Since the time we were in love

7

The End

Scrolls

If you don't understand by now
that all the standard rules got us here
that all the science,
doctors,
machines,
and even prophets
only seek to keep us here,
then I pray you'll be protected
as your eyes are opened so wide
that you can feel the sludge of your brain
leaking out of them;
and that you will escape to a long sleep;
and I pray that when you awaken,
you will have forgotten all you were told,
and only remember all that you are.

The Music Man

Out there driving
drastic measures
like
clappin' off-beats in 5/4 time
like
an angel army ranger
busy drawing up the frontlines
like
How you lay down & still time
& then fill it up with more you
& even time loves that thrill
of stretching open for your will

Now somehow you're getting even better
like better better know it, right?
Like
truthfully the heat between us
has been killing all these cold nights.

Thank you. Love you too.

FOR ALL INQUIRIES CONTACT

JENIFERTOUSSANTLLC@GMAIL.COM

IG: @jeninsight

Made in United States
Troutdale, OR
07/21/2023

11457970R00054